The ERIE CANAL

BY WALTER LAPLANTE

Gareth Stevens
PUBLISHING

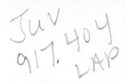
Please visit our website, www.garethstevens.com. For a free color catalog of all our high-quality books, call toll free 1-800-542-2595 or fax 1-877-542-2596.

Library of Congress Cataloging-in-Publication Data

Names: LaPlante, Walter, author.
Title: The Erie Canal / Walter LaPlante.
Description: New York : Gareth Stevens Publishing, [2017] | Series: Road
  trip: famous routes | Includes bibliographical references and index.
Identifiers: LCCN 2016001336 | ISBN 9781482446746 (pbk.) | ISBN 9781482449556 (library bound) | ISBN
9781482449440 (6 pack)
Subjects: LCSH: Erie Canal (N.Y.)–Juvenile literature. | Erie Canal
  (N.Y.)–History–Juvenile literature.
Classification: LCC HE396.E6 L36 2017 | DDC 386/.48/09747–dc23
LC record available at http://lccn.loc.gov/2016001336

First Edition

Published in 2017 by
Gareth Stevens Publishing
111 East 14th Street, Suite 349
New York, NY 10003

Copyright © 2017 Gareth Stevens Publishing

Designer: Andrea Davison-Bartolotta
Editor: Kristen Nelson

Photo credits: Cover, p. 1 debra millet/Shutterstock.com; cover, p. 1 © iStockphoto.com/catnap72; p. 4
Richard A. McGuirk/Shutterstock.com; p. 5 Barefoot_Photos/iStock/Thinkstock; p. 6 Fotosearch/Stringer/Getty Images;
p. 7 Joseph Sohm/Shutterstock.com; p. 8 Underwood Archives/Archive Photos/Getty Images; p. 9 Everett Historical/
Shutterstock.com; pp. 11 (map), 21 Rosemary Wardley/Munion/Wikimedia Commons; p. 11 (background) nikonphotog/
iStock/Thinkstock; p. 13 Emily Riddell/Lonely Planet Images; p. 15 MyLoupe/UIG/Universal Images Group/
Getty Images; p. 16 BRUCEPIX.COM/Shutterstock.com; p. 17 jiawangkun/Shutterstock.com; p. 18 Aspen Photo/
Shutterstock.com; p. 19 (both) Richard McGuirk/iStock/Thinkstock; p. 20 Matt Champlin/Moment Open/Getty Images.

Printed in the United States of America

CPSIA compliance information: Batch #CS16GS: For further information contact Gareth Stevens, New York, New York at 1-800-542-2595.

Contents

Words in the glossary appear in **bold** type the first time they are used in the text.

Waterway to the West

During the 1700s and early 1800s, the largest part of the US population lived on the East Coast. This was partly due to how costly and hard it was to move goods from the East Coast to territories further **inland**. The idea that a man-made waterway could solve this problem was first written about in 1807.

Over the next 10 years, the idea grew into the plans for the Erie **Canal**! It would connect the Hudson River, which leads to the Atlantic Ocean, and the Great Lakes.

Pit Stop

New York State governor DeWitt Clinton was one of the main supporters of the building of the Erie Canal.

All About the  Erie Canal

where found: New York State

year built: building began in 1817 and was completed in 1825

length: 363 miles (584 km)

cities along the canal: Buffalo, Rochester, Syracuse, Utica, Albany

major attractions: locks, Hudson River valley, the Finger Lakes, nearby canals, many historic sites, and parks

Today, the Erie Canal is a great place to take a road trip! Whether you're interested in history or nature, there's a lot to do.

Digging the Canal

When construction of the Erie Canal began in 1817, several groups were in charge of digging parts of the canal. However, across the 363 miles (584 km) that needed to be dug, there were several **elevation** changes. Something would need to help boats move from one water level to another as the land dipped and rose beneath the canal.

Engineers working on the project solved the problem with 83 stone locks! They also built 18 **aqueducts** so the canal could cross other bodies of water.

A lock is a closed area in a canal used to raise or lower boats as they pass from one water level to another by adding or taking away water. Today, the Erie Canal has 35 locks.

Pit Stop

Lockport, New York, is named for its Erie Canal locks! The two locks there still aid boats moving through an elevation change of 50 feet (15 m).

Success!

Once finished, the Erie Canal connected Lake Erie in Buffalo, New York, with Albany, New York. There, the waterway met the Hudson River, and boats could reach the Atlantic Ocean. Horses or mules pulled boats by walking on paths along the canal.

The canal was an instant success. It cut the cost of moving goods from Buffalo to New York City from $100 for each ton to $10! Supplies could make it to the Great Lakes **region** more quickly and easily—and that meant more people could settle there!

Pit Stop

The Erie Canal became a vacation spot for wealthy people in addition to a waterway for shipping!

The Erie Canal and life along it has become part of many stories and songs. Bruce Springsteen even recorded a song called "Erie Canal," based on a song written around 1905!

Canal Cities

Many of the main cities and towns in New York State are found along the Erie Canal. Buffalo, found on the eastern shore of Lake Erie, grew as a shipping center after the canal was completed because of its location at the western end of the canal.

Rochester, Syracuse, Utica, and the many other places grew during the canal's most successful years in the 1800s. If you visit any of these places, you can easily find a place to walk along the canal!

Pit Stop

New York City isn't on the canal, but it benefited greatly from it. It became the busiest port in the United States within 15 years of the canal opening.

From Buffalo (pictured below), goods were sent to Ohio, Illinois, Michigan, and Canada.

Shipping Changes

During the early 1900s, New York State made the canal deeper and wider so bigger ships could travel on it. But the changes weren't enough. Much of the canal's business started going to the railroads, and later, to another man-made waterway called the St. Lawrence Seaway. By the early 1960s, the canal wasn't used for trade much anymore.

Since then, it's become a great place to visit! Along much of the canal's length, the towing paths have been refinished and parks have been established nearby.

Pit Stop

Between 1823 and 1828, other canals were built connecting to the Erie Canal. Today, the Erie, the Champlain, the Oswego, and the Cayuga-Seneca Canals make up the New York State Canal System.

Many people enjoy boating on the Erie Canal. Visitors can sometimes take boat rides along different parts of it.

Around the Finger Lakes

The area around the Erie Canal is full of rolling hills, lovely lakes, and forests. It runs through some of the most beautiful parts of New York State.

The Finger Lakes are a group of lakes found near Rochester and Syracuse, New York. They're a popular road trip **destination**, especially during the summer. Visitors can enjoy nature and visit the Montezuma Wildlife Refuge. They can also stop at one of the many museums found in the region, including the Strong National Museum of Play!

Pit Stop

Seneca Falls, New York, isn't far from the Erie Canal. It was where the first women's rights **convention** took place and is home to the Women's Rights National Historic Park today.

When it was very active, the Erie Canal would close during the cold, snowy winter months. But summers in the region around the Erie Canal are commonly warm and sunny, including near lakes like this one.

Roosevelt on the Hudson

If you follow the Erie Canal east to Albany, there are even more fun road trip stops! Albany is in the northern part of the Hudson River valley, which then reaches down to New York City.

One important historic place to visit in the Hudson River valley is the home, presidential library, and museum of Franklin D. Roosevelt. Roosevelt so loved this region that he once said, "All that is within me cries out to go back to my home on the Hudson River."

Pit Stop

Post

Roosevelt's home is called Hyde Park. Visitors can tour the house where the only four-term US president lived!

Hyde Park

Albany is the state capital of New York. The capitol building has been used for state government since the 1880s and can be toured by visitors.

Biking the Canal

In many places along the Erie Canal, the towpaths have been kept up and **paved** for runners, hikers, and bicyclists. It's a great way for families to get out of the car to do something fun outside when stuck in a car on a road trip!

In addition, every year a group of bicyclists rides 400 miles (644 km) across New York State along the canal. They commonly ride about 50 miles (80 km) a day as they travel between Buffalo and Albany.

Pit Stop

Post

Sports fans can head southeast of the Erie Canal to Cooperstown, New York, to see the National Baseball Hall of Fame.

Whether you like to walk, run, or bike, a stop along the Erie Canal is a great place to get active!

Adopt a Trail

The state of New York and local governments are often in charge of taking care of the paths and parks around the Erie Canal. But **volunteers** do their part, too!

Why not do some community service along the Erie Canal as part of your road trip? The Adopt-a-Trail program matches families and groups with about a mile of trail along the Erie Canal. They clean up trash, clip bushes, fix the surface of the trail, and put up signs.

Pit Stop

There are many museums along the Erie Canal that tell its history. The Erie Canal Museum in Syracuse is housed in the only **weighlock** building left in the United States.

What To Do Along the Erie Canal

The Erie Canal Museum
Syracuse, NY

The Strong National Museum of Play
Rochester, NY

take an Erie Canal boat ride

Lake Ontario

- Oswego
- Niagara Falls
- Lockport
- Rochester
- Present route of Erie Canal
- Rome
- Syracuse
- Buffalo
- Seneca Falls
- Cooperstown
- Waterford
- Albany

CANADA

Lake Erie

Genesee River

Cayuga Lake

Seneca Lake

Susquehanna R.

Hudson River

NEW YORK

VERMONT

MASSACHUSETTS

hike, bike, or run along the towpaths

The National Baseball Hall of Fame
Cooperstown, NY

Women's Rights National Historic Park
Seneca Falls, NY

Glossary

aqueduct: a passage that's made to carry water

canal: a man-made waterway

convention: a gathering of people who have a common interest or purpose

destination: the place to which somebody or something is going

elevation: height above sea level

engineer: someone who plans and builds machines

inland: to the inner parts of a country

pave: to cover with concrete or other surface to make a path smooth and firm enough to travel on

region: a large area of land that has features that make it different from nearby areas of land

volunteer: a person who works without being paid

weighlock: a lock on a canal in which boats are weighed

For More Information

Books

Aller, Susan Bivin. *What Difference Could a Waterway Make? And Other Questions About the Erie Canal.* Minneapolis, MN: Lerner Publications, 2011.

Sahgal, Lara, and Janey Levy. *A Primary Source Investigation of the Erie Canal.* New York, NY: Rosen Publishing, 2016.

Thompson, Linda. *Building the Erie Canal.* Vero Beach, FL: Rourke Educational Media, 2013.

Websites

Building the Erie Canal
pbslearningmedia.org/resource/adlit08.ush.exp.erie/building-the-erie-canal/
Watch a video about the history of the Erie Canal.

Cycling for Kids
eriecanalway.org/explore/cycling/cycling-kids
Find some fun routes along the Erie Canal you can bicycle with family and friends!

Index